"Hetherington is…a witty, cosmopolitan but never affected writer, with a meticulous ear and an intellect matched to his technical skills. *Six Different Windows* is one the finest collections of poetry this year."—PETER PIERCE, The *Age*

"[T]he writing is at once simple and complex, beautiful and disturbing. These are poems to sink into, poems that are carefully crafted, born through experience and observation/intelligence, poems that deserve rereading and contemplation."—ROBYN CADWALLADER, *Verity La*

"This is poetry of glowing sensuality, of urgent narrative pace, of tact in its exploration of intimate experience. Hetherington is an important poet with a growing national and international reputation, and this is some of his most accomplished work."—SHIRLEY WALKER, *Australian Book Review*

"It is the sense of working for and with the whole poem…that marks Hetherington off from many other poets of his generation."—VIVIAN SMITH, *Southerly*

"This accomplished volume is the kind of poetry which will provoke thought on all those shared human experiences that matter."—ROD MORAN, The *West Australian*

"…his style is similarly lucid in voice, diction and image. This felicitous combination gives his poems the feel of poise, intelligence, grace and finish."—PAUL KANE, *Australian Book Review*

"…Hetherington's skill as a poet furnishes him with the tools to allow the reader a rich engagement …"—JOHN MATEER, The *Canberra Times*

"Paul Hetherington's poems conjure the power of words, not just in the way he uses them, but in the way he invokes the visceral nature of language, the sheer gutsiness of writing."—TOM GRIFFITHS

"Hetherington's writing is immaculate; he finds the hidden nuances at the core of each person…A beautiful piece of writing, to savour."—GLENDA GUEST, *Muse*

"Imaginative depth, crystallised moments, and finely conceived metaphors make this…an enchanting read."—MERLE GOLDSMITH, *Island*

Previous poetry collections by Paul Hetherington

Books
Acts Themselves Trivial (1991)
The Dancing Scorpion (1993)
Shadow Swimmer (1995)
Canvas Light (1998)
Stepping Away: Selected Poems (2001)
Blood and Old Belief: A Verse Novel (2003)
It Feels Like Disbelief (2007)
Six Different Windows (2013)
Watching the World: Impressions of Canberra (2015) (with Jen Webb)

Chapbooks
Mapping Wildwood Road (1990)
Chicken and Other Poems (2012)
Viscera (2014)
Jars (2015)

Publications accompanying exhibitions
Spectral Resemblances (2013) (with Anita Fitton)

BURNT UMBER

Paul Hetherington has previously published nine full-length collections of poetry, including *Six Different Windows* (UWA Publishing), along with four poetry chapbooks. He won the 2014 Western Australian Premier's Book Awards (poetry) and the 1996 Australian Capital Territory Book of the Year Award; and was a finalist in the 2012, 2013 and 2014 international *Aesthetica* Creative Writing Competitions. He was shortlisted for the 2013 Newcastle Poetry Prize and the 2013 Montreal International Poetry Prize. Recently he was awarded an Australia Council for the Arts Residency at the BR Whiting Studio in Rome, and in 2012 he was awarded one of two places on the Australian Poetry Tour of Ireland. In 2002 he was the recipient of a Chief Minister's ACT Creative Arts Fellowship. His poems have been published in anthologies, journals, magazines and on websites in a variety of countries. He edited the final three volumes of the National Library of Australia's authoritative four-volume edition of the diaries of the artist Donald Friend (volume four was shortlisted for the Manning Clark House 2006 National Cultural Awards) and was founding editor of the Library's quarterly humanities and literary journal *Voices* (1991–97). He is head of the International Poetry Studies Institute (IPSI) in the Centre for Creative and Cultural Research at the University of Canberra, where he is Professor of Writing in the Faculty of Arts and Design, and he is one of the founding editors of the international online journal *Axon: Creative Explorations.*

BURNT UMBER

PAUL HETHERINGTON

UWA PUBLISHING

First published in 2016 by
UWA Publishing
Crawley, Western Australia 6009
www.uwap.uwa.edu.au

UWAP is an imprint of UWA Publishing
a division of The University of Western Australia

THE UNIVERSITY OF
WESTERN
AUSTRALIA

National Library of Australia Cataloguing-in-Publication entry:
Hetherington, Paul, 1958– author.
Burnt umber / Paul Hetherington.
ISBN: 9781742588063 (paperback)
Australian poetry.
A821.3

Cover image: "The Secret Life of Trees", 2012 (detail) by Judith Crispin
Cover design by Upside Creaative
Typeset in Bembo by Lasertype
Printed by Lightning Source

This project has been assisted by the Australian Government
through the Australia Council, its arts funding and advisory body.

Australian Government

Australia
Council
for the Arts

uwapublishing

For my father,
Robert (Bob) Hetherington (1923–2015)

"…deep shining ochres, burnt umber and parchments of baked earth—reflecting on itself and through itself, filtering the light."

—Tom Stoppard, *Rosencrantz and Guildenstern are Dead*

"And then you are a studied brightness of thought.
You stumble, and are a gathering of question marks,
like a flotilla of boats, a penned group of deer;
you are a questing adventure and a dark full-stop,
an earthly angel bodied out by doubt.
Your shyness is a continuing joust with yourself
hardly mediated by those you know;
you're a dancer who unlearned his early steps,
a lyric performer whose lyre would not sing out."

"…all ekphrasis is notional, and seeks to create a specific image that is to be found only in the text as its 'resident alien,' and is to be found nowhere else."

—WJT Mitchell, *Picture Theory: Essays on Verbal and Visual Representation*

Contents

Pictures at an exhibition 1

Painting 1: *Burnt Umber*

The clock blanks, and blanks again.
Paintings step from walls,
moving into the room.
Ticking stops; paint spreads
like a bordello's red light.
I'm part of a scene
where a man in bowler hat
pats a green dog.
There's a turquoise mist,
a slug on a window
and barking as the man nods "hello".
I look back towards the bedroom—
it could be my wife
but the image is blurred.
The painting flattens me.
The slug trails slime;
the dog drags at my trouser leg
and is turning blue.
A burnt umber grin eats its mouth.

Painting 2: *Gunship*

His face might be frowning
or briefly possessed
by spasms of knowledge,
his arms akimbo
like a tightrope exotic
wheeling past crowds.
There's an asphalt road
reaching toward
a knot in the hills—
five children climb
to a mosque or small church.
A gunship is circling.
A splash of black paint
explodes in a cornfield.
There's no goodly view
to throw this scene
into stable perspective.
A man near a shop
faces the wall
with white, skewered arms.

You have known
this brick-and-wood town—
buildings are squat;
windows sit high
near the brow of cafe;
the street climbs
into eels of thin light;
there's a small figure
in yellow and blue.
Three ghostly others
carouse in swirls
of pallor, brown.
I've lived there, too,
in a life not revealed—
crossing this street
in a different year,
looking for you—
your green scarf and coat
and quick, seeking gait—
but found only absence
as if, after all,
the place was just paint,
as if in departure
you stepped into pigments
the painter forgot.

Painting 4: *Doppelgänger*

This painting's my doppelgänger,
stealing what I thought was mine alone.
Eerily, it knows me like a brother,
scooping lymph and blood
with palette knife and brushes,
bringing into view
instances that never have cohered.
The painter scraped at surfaces to yield
a peeled, tender consciousness
permeating unframed dimensions
more surely than I walk about this room
(all clean lines and depth;
all composition and achieved perspective).
In the painting I am scattered,
settling nowhere, recollection skewed
like light skittering from a broken globe.

Painting 5: *Magpies*

Six magpies
wait, backs to the viewer—
wild rhythms of creatures
in close-seated parlay
watching dense light
and rivers express
an ancient, encoded
flex and spin.
The painting sees them
black-hued and glossy,
looking like hussars
in the old glory days.

Painting 6: *Eyes*

for BL

A hundred eyes
examine me like an insect,
red and yellow like fear.
What walks about me
in dirty boots, holding my ideas
ridiculous? Whose face
visits restless nights,
threatening to blank my dreams—
a near-perfect oval and no-colour;
obliteration like a smile?
The painting becomes a murder
of Aztec nobility in the Temple
and time droning
through aeons of absence,
away from a ripe papaya
lined with a hundred black eyes,
delicate and full as prayer.
The painting folds back into wind.
Brushes, palette knife,
insouciant pigments
vanish into drawers;
the painting becomes the green
of your scarf,
its future tucked
out of sight. It nods
and a hundred eyes blink.
There is nowhere
that doesn't watch me.

Painting 7: *Running Girl*

for RT

Harum–scarum
a girl runs through the wood
and the painting embraces her form,
sucking it into canvas and white ground
as if to absorb every colour
of hair, cloak, decorated bonnet;
as if to hold her name, in secret.
"Annabel" proclaims the painting
"in the Wild Wood", but her true name lives
in some guttural sound
that speaks ancient knowledge
against inflections
of time and society.
She knows herself
sliding between shadows
saying "earth" and "escape"
as if calling her sisters.
The painting breathes her,
draping furniture with wildness,
a horned creature
among evening's clamour.

Painting 8: *Bank*

It is not used to me.
I grasp clenched sides
and fingers encounter
stiff-backed resistance.
I stare at the surface—
all mottled, dark hues.
Figures have vanished
since yesterday morning;
silence has varnished
every untoward claim
they made on my house.
But a colour sits up
like a boy at the edge
of a roseate dam
and black ducks go skywards.
The boy's lying
on a crumble-edged bank
where water sucks clay
like a wet kind of smoke.
His shirt is the blue
of a delicate vein
at the top of a thigh
and when he stands tall
the blood of his hair
in the day's afterglow
is arterial.

Painting 9: *Postures*

Because the painting never sleeps;
because it faces the hallway
and its images
are always sneaking into the house;
because it leaves a scent
of mint and coriander;
because it's always on the verge of speaking
but never mouths a word,
and despite this, is replete
with gnomic utterance;
because it's protean and colludes
with the rhythms of hours and seasons
and seems a little shamefaced every morning;
because it's unmannered
yet full of its own postures
like nine circus performers
claiming attention at once;
because it's sometimes funny
but also an elegy
for lost, unnameable things;
I have sometimes wondered,
when insomniac in bed,
what the hallway hears.

Painting 10: *Dismay*

The model has gone,
stepping out of paint,
gathering her robes.
The floor where they lay
is a luminous patch
of scrubbed, bare boards—
sun trails fingers,
searching for soft
and slippery satin
but finds only dust motes
that can't be held.
The picture gazes
in acute dismay
like a face without nose,
for she was its feature,
undressed and bathing—
like an ancient nymph
but with new attitude.
I hold her in thought
walking through woodland,
dressed, unwatched.

Rooftop: a prose poetry sequence

Rooftop

for JS

1.

The rooftop he has since lost was a place of assignation. He took a vaporetto through intimacies of canals—it was a key turning the city's lock; a hand negotiating an unfamiliar arm.

2.

As he ducked under the strangely low doorway and listened to rain, she said there'd be a rooftop party; that they should go. "Tomorrow," she said. She peeled an orange, its skin curling like boats on the canal. He leant towards her but resisted placing his palms upon her face. He watched rain banging on cobblestones. "I've found a balcony apartment," she said. He shrugged, feeling his vacation becoming his life, like something unknown in the air, a yellow and green scent.

3.

They walked and water was a hundred discolourations of memory. It irked him—not to be able to let her go, even now. His present companion looked away into the lagoon and pointed. Memory grasped him like a third person. It said something about smell; about how he'd loved the watery, staining smell of her. His companion turned. "Are you listening?" "Of course." It might have been something the wind uttered. It might have been something spoken by the canal.

4.

In the yard of the gallery names of dead dogs were pressed against a wall—a story of how memory persuades us of its purposes. Inside, he was moved by abstract paintings that had no more narrative than poems, sucking away time like portals into absence. Or, was that presence—the not-backward-not-forward-looking moments of these canvases? His companion praised a yellow image and he immediately began to care for her more, as if a door opened between them. He laid a hand on the image as he had earlier imagined laying hands on her face. A guard said "no." Eyes wandered towards him in the painting's flat depths.

5.

He wondered again what he'd cared for. The mysteries of skin were an inordinate puzzle—sensations like present-remembering and fulfilment-in-loss. Desire inhabiting irretrievable things and names lacquering them. His companion pointed to a painting's skin-coloured pink. He thought of frangipanis. "It's the colour of love," she said.

6.

What he found in the water was his own disappointment looking up, waxwork-like, from a sift of currents. "Why do you need to walk alone?" She took his arm; shepherding him back into an idea of a life together. He thought of that Etruscan sculpture of a man and woman sitting together, encouched. Water lapped like a thousand whispering tongues. He listened to her heartbeat on his palm.

7.

He climbed stairs and felt each one as a day passing under his feet. Stone, like obdurate feeling. Shadow, like failing knowledge. A sense of chiaroscuro as if he was painted into a fixed Renaissance view. Lenslike light sucked his body towards the rooftop but the spiral he climbed turned away. Eventually he heard the hubbub and remembered she'd be there, her slim white arms emblematic of beauty. Yet his knowledge of her was meagre as the catch from yesterday's canal. Old water; two silver and squirming slippages of light. Stale ends of the sea.

8.

He wondered how there could be so many stairs. A girl let him in, a man with a tray offered a liquid kaleidoscope—he chose a red jar and held it like a heart in his hand. After the music, after hijinks and conversation, he watched morning steep old buildings in watery stains. They stood like glory's vestige; he thought he saw an empire stand up. So much commerce, so many wide and humming sails, Astor Piazzolla's *Oblivion* wafting across water.

9.

Undertow. It was a hand with a white ring. Fingers worrying it. Words as if dropped from air, bothering the mind like flies. How had this...? From her black diamante bag she pulled an envelope that he wouldn't read; that he threw away. Two years of confusion. A thousand necklaced sentences of justification—his and hers. The envelope floated towards the canal. "What did you write?" he said.

10.

When she clamped her mouth to his mouth he could neither speak nor sing and wondered whether she was suppressing laughter. Later they walked by the canal. On the rooftop Piazzolla had given way to Handel's *Water Music*. She spoke of art and meaning but he refused to understand her, remembering similar words from someone else. Then he'd believed, wanting art's ineffable transport. Yet she'd abandoned him like any other affair...Now he said goodbye. She stayed and the rooftop beckoned; music was shifting again, like wind. She had him by the collar.

11.

On the rooftop she fell with a glass and a ruby baubled on her wrist. He helped her up but her eyes were a discoloured glaze as if they, too, might crack. Their beauty almost blanked, like a clock's hands vanishing in striking the hour; a house falling into brick and rubble from superb architectural grace. Hours, centuries pass as he knows less and less. She's unconscious in other hands as the old city breathes vapours. He sees nothing of the canal—the famous view he came for—and the waiter pours pale liquid. His glass brims with emptiness.

12.

Days later the rooftop vanished, as if reality had shifted a degree. Doorways looked the same but led to manicured gardens. He found himself facing the wrong way. In a cloister girls were practising for a band, marching up and down paving stones. They wore clothes like foliage of exotic trees. At last, he thought, clambering up a familiar fire escape, but the door was closed. Three weeks puzzling it out, wading through crowds, establishing sight lines.

A woman he met at a party said she'd be his guide. They climbed a stairway and faced unfamiliar water. She teased him that one rooftop was as good as another but he wouldn't stay, realising that the city was escaping him, like a Behemoth rippling its flanks.

13.

She had shrugged: "Words; after all, they were only words. When I said 'always', I meant 'for at least another month'. When I said 'enamoured' it was a temporary idea." The canal was murky with millions of dropped words and misunderstandings. They'd walked to a cafe and eaten *spaghetti alle vongole*, talking of memory's long strands. She'd held up spaghetti on a fork—"like this. All those soft connections of time and affection." It had seemed funny, as a vaporetto with entwined lovers cruised past, flustering water. "Language is almost all for me," she'd said. "But how does one know what one means?"

14.

A woman found a letter caught in a pot plant's foliage. A cream envelope with embossing; paper that reminded her of working at the embassy. There was no address and she opened it. "I would like to..." Pages discussing love and friendship, like a long walk through hilly country. Details she looked away from, watching sluggish water sidle and twist. "I wanted you but..."—a logic of the heart. "It was superb and yet..."—a catch in the letter's breath. "It changed my life but I cannot do it now"—a phrase like a chime on wind. She glanced up, sure she'd heard a bell or a voice. She wondered who had written, who was yet to read. "Dear Ian" gave no useful clue. The letter was signed "M".

15.

He finally found the rooftop the day before leaving. The way was not as he remembered. If it were skin, it would have been raw; a stiff wind blew across its surface. Fragments of glass remained and a scarf caught on a railing, streaming like Rapunzel's hair. He recollected her fingers idling on the glass, as if possessing a tune. Sheet music flapped, pinned to a wall. What had he encountered, Piazzolla seeming to cry his name? He listened and heard nothing. Yet a ghost had left his body and was consorting there.

16.

He had been listening to Callas sing *Tosca* and the opening of the final act tolled like his own heart. How stars had certainly shone, he thought—slippery as balls of mercury—when the rooftop gaped like wounded memory and the woman he saw stood like another he'd loved. When his own face had been that of a Pierrot—even he had observed an inherent and trusting foolishness. Yet he'd carried on, caught up in his own intrigue. Now cut waterlily flowers were gawping mouths. The libretto entered his body; no other words were possible.

17.

He stood on the rooftop for the last time. Concrete rot, absence everywhere, as if air were resuming the building while, below, the palazzo leaned into the canal. He remembered the letter. A woman had advertised—"Envelope found, addressed to Ian". She'd blushed, "yes, I read it. I couldn't help myself." He read it, too, in front of her as she poured tea and proferred biscuits: "A difficult time?" She was as discreet and blunt as a docking gondola. "Yes," he said. "I loved her and she thought better of it." They exchanged pleasantries, sharing a third party's intimate language; almost kissing, both thinking better of it. She handed him a card: "Ring me?" The rooftop showed a view into a wide apartment. A woman was undressing a man.

Angels at
Nedlands Primary School

Angels at Nedlands Primary School, 1968

Sunlight saturated walls
of our year-five classroom
with end-of-April yellow
and a blur of angels.
As Mrs Fry recited collective nouns
bottles in the milk shed
fizzed and exploded
and the headmaster
entered the school grounds
in boxer shorts. His P.A., Mrs Lesley
sobbed into an ice-cream cone—
"a lake," someone said,
"to go with her bonsai pines."
Angels sauntered through the cafeteria.
It was nearly time for P.E.
so we were ushered to the bottom oval
where hymns began to climb
from the purplish tangle
of prunus next to the girls toilets
and Jenny Carruthers announced
that her palms were bleeding.
By now angels were in the garden,
uprooting roses, their wings
shining like taffeta.
Jenny knelt on the asphalt.
The deputy headmistress
strode across the oval
as angels demolished the gardener's shed.
They ascended slowly
as in a Raphael painting.
The headmaster quit his job
for "personal reasons",
the chair of school council
inspected damage
and Jenny showed scars
of her stigmata for weeks,

removing shoes and socks
during lessons. A few of us
looked for the angels to return
throughout years six and seven
and, once, a friend said
they were at the swimming pool
but all we saw was a drunk
collapsed on blue tiles—
though it's true that small wings
sprouted from his shoulders.
Just before graduation we made a pact
to keep faith, despite general scepticism.
"Angels don't exist", a teacher said,
giving us detention.

Fox

That day, in his yard,
herding cattle for drenching—
all that slop and kicked wet—
a bony fox trotted
away from the henhouse,
blood on its orange
like a gash in beauty.

He knew what he'd find
but dawdled in going,
hefting a spade,
twisting beans like clusters
of tangled sinkers
from triangulations
of tight, leaning pickets.

The hens were a mess
and he buried them quickly,
dispatching one
that was twitching and beaking,
shrugging anger
away from shoulders.

Later that day, as cattle fed,
he jumped the creek
where he often caught yabbies,
remembering hoisting
his wife and child
out of a flood,
joining young saplings
with a wrist-thick towrope.
The perished rope
was high in the canopy
and dark with lost seasons.

A woman he'd met
when buying horse blankets
had come for five weeks.
Every still evening
they'd watched grey teals
skim the low dam
and the wedge-shaped white
of their underwing.

In last week's post
he'd received a snapshot—
"something to keep
of that sweet holiday"
and "sorry I won't
be seeing you soon"—
two of them smiling
at camera and tripod,
a fox behind them
crossing cleared ground.

Bushfire

Tumultuous, for months
the aftermath of fire—
burnt stumps, spindles of trees,
ash rising on the slightest wind,
wafting, sinking
like particles of memory,
nights charred with recollection,
cries chasing conversations,
and incalescent weather
like 40 days of sunstroke
darkening the district.
The local store piled its verandah
with new goods,
stashed beer and milk
in its freezers. Its generator groaned
and, where the fire had caught it,
its west side leaned
into black-toothed grimace.
Someone picked up Jimmy's kite
twenty kilometres from the township.
Someone else wrote letters
to every politician in the district.
A teenage girl was seen
by three men walking
on the road out of town
although no girl lived there.
Rain came in drops like stones
clagging ash, banging roofs,
making molten dreams.

House
for HRS

He always lived there—
on plum-red escalations of morning
when magpies warbled from fence-posts
and heat ran like streamers through the living room;
during mild winters when rain clagged windows
and someone drew stick figures
of copulating buffalo on sweating glass.
He picked a bougainvillea spike from loping couch grass
and tickled his sister's feet with its point
as she rolled and squealed.
He circumnavigated his parents' bedroom
where arguments like smoke snuck under the heavy door.
They emerged shadowed by make-up,
buying Neapolitan ice cream at the local deli
where Mr Georgiades said "Soon nobody will have to die."
He couldn't believe that
because birds sometimes fell from the air
and his parents inhabited death like a promise of final satisfaction,
their loose bones and flesh seductive
with the knowledge of growing old.
The house was ransacked in his indolent games
by Roman soldiers who made its stones
as slippery as egg-whites, and was finally cut in half
on a day when smoke hovered over the suburb,
a hundred ghosts exiting walls
and sliding from floorboards that twisted and groaned.
It was lifted like a Leviathan in two exposed sections
with furniture taped to its ribs,
and trundled on a truck through dust
like clouds of unknowing.
He was pressed tight to those walls
or running for cover as his father walked with a belt
wrapped tightly around knuckles.
His sister leered from her corner bedroom
where the louvres were open and a boy was looking in,
saying "You're in for it now."

There was a smell of rising yeast
and his mother's high voice broke as if she'd been crying.
Crows cawed, settling
on exposed, unsteady ground.

Furniture

Furniture we'd shared
sat between us—
stools, tables,
rugs that flattened the floor—
and days, squalls of cloud.
Everything meant distance;
skies shifted colour;
at different windows
air ran like pennants.
Words baulked at spaces
we'd filled with speaking,
departing like squadrons
of black-and-yellow insects.
They left a faint shadow;
a colouring like fur.
On some days
intimacy was a trapeze artist,
clambering on ropes
out into distance,
the Big Top gathering
humid breathing.
After she descended,
her sequins winking,
pressed against air,
vestigial astonishment
crowded her absence,
a chair you had liked
growing ungainly
as a vine in a hothouse.

A Museum of the Future

"In that time—hard to believe, I know—
millions of people crowded ugly cities
yet were barely joined. They often lived
in ruinous relationships called marriages—
a bargaining of distrust and plain contempt,
making use of devices they called phones—
monstrous things that barely even fitted
their unprogrammed hands."

                  The mind-script paused,
conveyed a modest smile, and said "Caress
was quite unguided. They made it up
as mood and occasion took them, often failing
to bring real pleasure to the one they touched."

There was laughter in the group.

                  "Hard to imagine—
they would be alone with personal thoughts
for many hours. Some made art or wrote
the poetry you see in that display.
And see the pulp of paper they called a book.
They also suffered as the outcasts do—
believers in free will and common lies
about individual consciousness—
a strange idea that everyone can be
separate from the proud community."

The digital diorama showed a scene
where people sat in rooms and watched a screen.
"They did a lot of that to pass the time,
only fifty years ago and yet
not so different from the ancient Romans
who liked their baths and comfort, and constructed
roads, and aqueducts to channel water.
To see that mini-drama, turn left now."

Refugees

1.
In later days
doctors marvelled
at the prevalence of self-harm;
people uttered
unwieldy lamentations;
guards escorted men
to noiseless rooms.
Days flattened into textures
of threadbare cloth;
children stared
at unkempt horizons.
The law said
they were to be emptied
and despatched to islands;
rote statements of process
demanded that letters
be blacked out or burned.
Regularly herded
into antiseptic rooms,
shifted between compounds,
some made appeals
but judgments
crowded them like warders.
Often when they woke at night
they saw obliteration
like a beast
examining their prospects.

2.
Three men with names
that guards can't pronounce—

close, intimate syllables
with which their parents
caressed them.

And they won't give
those syllables away
even though their identities
have been shredded
like unwanted documents;
even though others
are carried away
and brought back.

They have travelled from places
where people traded in markets
and children stood on tiptoe
pointing at sweets.

At night they sense
someone bending over their beds.

In the morning they know
they have five more times to die.

3.
His daughter became silent
as if an intolerable gesture
had climbed into her eyes.
She neither looked at him
nor towards distance,
dancing a few steps
for hours at a time.
No-one joined her
for fear that the rhythm
would graft to their bodies.
Guards ignored her, doctors agreed
"there'd been some trauma".
Week by week she unravelled
in abrasive circles
as men sewed their lips
to protest. She was in the yard
when someone pushed her,
trying to undo
her goading
travail of movement.

River

There was never an explanation
as to why he walked into the river,
took hold of a log
and floated away.
They found letters
but the love he expressed
in sometimes obsessive detail
was no explanation—
except, the coroner declared
that perhaps it indicated
"a lack of a grasp", etc.
Someone who saw him pass by
said that he was waterlogged;
another said he sat upright,
as if triumphant, and was singing;
a third (unreliable) party
stated that he rolled and turned
and was having trouble breathing.
The coroner said that "unless a body", etc.
And, certainly there was a report
that he had, after all, survived;
had walked out of the water
near a remote village.
"It sounds implausible," the witness said,
who was rather bedraggled himself
with downcast eye,
"but he seemed to be smiling,
if shaking a little—
and appeared to be looking at something
not so far in the distance.
You know, like a thought
can sometimes hold a man."

Ai Weiwei's *Table with Two Legs on the Wall*

Eyes anchor our world,
much as these legs
anchor a table
against the pale wall.
We walk with eyes
across the future's
intractable surface,
travelling incessantly
at ninety degrees
to what our feet know,
shifting perspective;
gathering angles
imagining ourselves
in unlikely places—
as if, at last
we might stand apart
from upright conviction
and flat, trodden ground.

Savasana

Decades sag and unfold—
we're both twenty
and straggles of river boulders
are greened with watermelon skins.
Four local children
wade back to stand
near a juddery bridge,
watching red triangulations
slant and fall sideways
on a sunlit plate.
We're visitors, confirming
an agreement to share
mountain water.

Birds drop and lift
in billows and crests.
An insect blurs to stillness
like unidentified thought,
leaves meander as rain.

You, my six-months' friend,
turn to face your past—
a narrative of riding
your town church's roof,
swaying outwards on shifting tiles,
slim and precocious
like a living saintly effigy:
"If only nuns were not denied relations."

We are driving; heat eats the land
with forebodings of ruthless futures.
In the mind's eye of conversation
my grandfather ploughs mallee country,
dragging scrub with a chain between tractors,
cropping, moving away.

Memory's weight holds his reverie:
death-staring war as a British pilot;
his mother's drowned body—
he was told an accident
but as a teenager found a newspaper report.

You interrupt and we follow a wetland trail,
ignoring arias of mosquitoes
and a possum scrabbling upwards
on a broken-branched eucalypt.
Phrases sit between us.
You gesture and they unfold from hands
like something bestowed.
We sense what was valued
when boundaries of creek and hill,
valley and stiff-backed ridge
were structures of language—
and even here, in these late days,
they're speaking us
into different constellations,

no longer belonging
on byways where weather
is often unkind—
as if, after all, the old, destructive gods
are again implicated in human unhappiness.
Words pause between us,
walking next to a water course.

We can't say it—
a susurration in our bodies;
something that belongs
to the silty river,
language falling so far into sensation
that its form begins to morph.

Perhaps there's a stone
we might take back
to remind us.

Savasana: deep breath;
fingers lying away; thoughts
settling, turning
in unruly new-becomings,
chasing light. Creek, pebbled flow,
a sensation of "rain",
the skating of leaf and insect;
finding cold words,
washing from them
soil and grey fungus; thoughts
as viscous brown sap;
a worm sitting
in a thick material of air.
Holding nothing
to what it has been;
a way of dying.

We return to our rented house
and a tree next to the driveway
like an image of complex thought—
unfurling foliage in forty-degree heat,
staying put through evolutions
of night-time and day.
After breakfast we walk outside
to gaze at its form
and something's lost
that neither of us utter—
our skins no longer
holding our bodies
in their usual postures.

A small lizard twists between rocks;
a bird sits on the roof
screeching at approaching bushfire.

We're ready to return.
We're unready to return.
Savasana.

Lung: prose poems

Lung

If the room was a lung, he was panting a little—exhausted from an effort he couldn't pin down. What had he been through? Windows breathed and did not break. The vista of the city stretched into ventricles and vessels. Buildings reddened with light; cars were crawling corpuscles. What did he know, except the failure of knowledge to put things right? And speaking's obduracy.

Dodgems

He knew her nascently, as if emotion was a gathering of strands; a site of momentum and possibility—where the future was conjured. He felt it as pain; a subtle chastisement; dark tropes of mind that would not be quietened. He heard a noise of dodgem cars, their buzz of small lightning. He felt the thigh of a girl, her breath forced against his ear in a clattering stall, backed sideways-forwards as she leaned over him to steady herself. It was all possibility, the future fingering his pocket.

Meringues

A smell of stewing apples. Meringues on a tray. His sister runs from outside. He looks up and sees his parents facing each other near the doorway. What do the closed hands mean in which his father's concentration has gathered? What are the stiff arms his mother holds as if she were a marionette? And words uttered one by one as if disconnected? His sister bites a meringue, its crumbs falling to the floor. He wants to gather them, but does nothing. There's nothing he can do.

Parlourmaid

Death was a parlourmaid dusting the mantelpiece on which sat a clock, an ornate box, an unopened envelope. Her eyes possessed no feeling as she gathered and wound day like ribbons. Light left the room; furniture sat teeteringly upright, eaten by woodworm. "I have done all I can," she remarked before leaving. Feeble light returned slowly. Furniture creaked and settled. Love held nothing at bay.

Rooms

for CA

1.

When you are in the desert and undulations of dunes slide toward you, you may remember a room. Under shiny stars, in the cold sweep of night, you'll hold that room close. And in blade-like morning, when light strikes the ground like scattered gemstones, you may stare at distance and know that room as if it were in your body—a place in which you're strong, no matter how small its dimensions. It is like a skin that knows the flow of your blood. It's where you discovered the value of limitation.

2.

Sometimes it contains a staircase; at other times it's small and spare, smelling of plum cake and tart cumquat liqueur spilled on linoleum. Occasionally it has ornate furniture and colourful half-pulled drapes. A boy hides behind a chest; a girl rubs a dress's green satin between fingers. A dog pants; a bath runs nearby. The girl stands on tiptoe, looking through a cobwebbed window. Later the boy sucks the inside of her thigh and she holds onto his hair. Sometimes the room is elongated, high in a building. There are dark floorboards; light squeezes through shutters.

3.

Rooms are informed by what's no longer there—light that wonders at you lying in a cot; space circling; dark drowning; walls like an unfixed firmament of mind. You grow up and forget those rooms but they cling; become stairs without end; an intimate boudoir of dreaming; a lit mystery behind doors— always old-fashioned, as if belonging to a different century. They are like early touch, haunting every exploration.

Paragraphs
for AR

Sharing no language, they met at a fruiterers gesticulating over apples and heads of lettuce. They pressed leaves, opened colours with palms of hands—three times, handling avocados gently as babies' skulls; gathering apricots in pincered fingers. They drank tea in a workshop one owned, began to plane wood and pore over diagrams. Drills showered sparks; metal slivered from clamps. Ten years later they had phrases and words in common—"yes", "no", "try it this way". Tables and benches were pages and paragraphs.

Gate

The cupboard held a pile of comics, and a second pile of magazines. It contained rat sack, tomato dust and a digging tool encrusted with earth. There were two letters in torn envelopes—one from a bank manager and another from "Abigail". She wrote in blue, ovoid letters that she expected something else. The letter was addressed to "Jack" with the comment "this time I nearly used your name". Hens ran free. A notice was nailed to the gate.

What Was Left

A towel and bathing cap remained, and a tattered copy of a novel: *The Red Room*. They belonged to 13-year-old Lena, his Swiss pen pal, who stayed for five weeks during a ferocious summer. Nearly every day his parents took them all to the beach—his sisters, friends, the next-door-neighbour's kids—where they ate canned beans on balmy evenings. An uncle took them to a riverfront resort. They played table tennis and quoits, swam in a long blue pool. Twelve years old, he felt shy, while his sisters kept company with their dolls. Lena made friends with older boys. Twice his uncle brought her back to the resort—but negligently, as if enjoying her truancy. On the last night someone saw her in a dinghy near the falls. Rescued, half-undressed, she left the next day. His mother would not speak to his uncle. The novel lay for months in the spare bedroom like a remonstration.

Five Occasions of Water

1. Sea

It lies on pale sand like an animal asleep, breathing slowly in its long dreaming. Surely nothing will wake it. Three boys enter its soft, excessive fur, and two girls follow, bobbing awkwardly. They are unflustered; parents call them in. Sun caresses and glares at it, but it does not wake. Night glosses its coat with knots and writhings of stars.

2. Peat Bog

He fell into her and began to disappear—slowly, like a man preserved in peat. What was left was a face searching for itself in extremity; exaggerated gestures of arms and hands. His days became a preoccupation with immersion; the sensation of being bathed. When released he disliked the feeling of air and freedom, permeated as he was by staining, tannic water. New words felt odd and dry in his mouth. Months later he still walked in damaged rags, living a solitude of what he no longer knew.

3. Houseboat

The flat water's surface gathers shadows as a houseboat creeps into a lock. Days, centuries stand under brows of houses. For a moment there's a crowd and cries of announcement; a man dangling arms in the stocks. It vanishes; slow silence is a hovering dragonfly. The houseboat drops as water rushes out. The boat's small garden shudders; a woman unwinds hair.

4. Ocean

At its deepest, we don't know it—what currents suck; what creatures may abide. Occasionally a fish like a species of night; a goggling surprise, straddles a plank of a trawler's deck. There's no way of naming what we have no noun for. Scientists would preserve it but fishermen throw it back. That released, sudden shudder.

5. Water

They fell out of him like water—words; emotions; stretched, elasticised thought. Years of knowledge dissolved and dissipated. His body was a thousand replayed events, every one spreading in liquefaction. The words were ordinary enough, despite hooks and wires, and their dissolution turned them to rust. He saw a figure in a mirror like a red-hued rainstorm.

Roadways

1.

In a room that overlooked a busy road they ate pasta with egg. Night was thick with traffic, strands of connection joined their bodies. Possibilities reached the quotidian; the real was said and held. Pasta on a fork. Time slipping through the tines. Words sticky in their believing mouths.

2.

A window looked onto a bent roadway, next to which a child stood staring at a black sky. Cars streamed towards suburbs distant as midday; a lightning strike burnt an outhouse. The child looked into her book, seeing the Milky Way, beginning to recite parables.

Music

It belongs nowhere, unless in a steep-roofed house at the back of town. A quartet might be in the lounge room, the slow movement enclosing two bodies. They are almost in love, yoking ideas in arms and legs. The music is glaring summer and an electrical storm. Later it will hold cool water, rhythms of days. A minor key is regret but the house doesn't notice. The future is low in the violins.

Heroes
for MH

They knew they had to die. The gods ordained it and all that followed were practicalities. Prepare slowly and with good conscience, fight hard, yield not a *daktylos* to the Persians. Remember one's comrades as one would wish to be remembered, even in battle's hideousness. Remember, too, one's lineage and home—women, children, the sacred places, but think of them lightly, with fondness like a breeze ruffling hair. Never think of the future.

Viscera: poems from WWII

Trench

They stood at the slit trench's edge
pissing nervously, ducking down.
Bombs, when they came,
were thumping exclusions of sense
as if language and thought
had lost all bearings,
thrown like dirt into air.
One man's memory:
a child standing upright in a ditch
being belted by his father,
red-faced, apoplectic.
Not far away bombs hit a trench
square on, men falling in bits
on scoured ground.
That red again. The way
the face pales at the end.

Sun Bursts

Explosions were not flowers
sun-bursting their way over fields,
but looked like improbable sea creatures
pulsing and blooming in a cycle of feeding.
Occasionally a barn or house was hit
and a section of it burnt
with a kind of belatedness,
or the whole thing vanished in conflagration.
Sometimes a person was ducking
and the sea anemone sucked them away
in a single movement.
Once or twice someone looked startled
as a bomb blossomed near them
and, afterwards, stood in a daze
hearing the surprise of their breathing.

Meeting

She greeted the man cautiously,
fed him, pointed the way to a border.
But he stayed, liking the tilt of her head
and her skirt riding on her buttocks.
She was surprised at his easy kindness;
and how he watched her
but, at first, was careful not to touch.
He helped bring up her son.
Two years later, as he dug in their garden,
three soldiers approached.
"Guten tag," raising guns.
He lowered his spade as she ran towards them,
shouting something in German.
The day was blue-skied
and he thought the soldiers were Russian;
that surely there was
an awkward misunderstanding.

Dropped Book

The dropped book lay on soil, its equations
partly obliterated by dirt. Later, he heard
that the boys were found in a ditch,
thrown like bags of grain. One had run
and two had stood quietly. All had been shot.
Their mother survived, living in the woods.
Every day she made an obeisance of sorts,
lighting a fire, nosing at the sky
like an animal, grunting and scratching.

Burning the Books

They packed into a truck
chairs with finely turned legs
and two or three paintings
of country life—showing a farm,
streams in a valley, a skipping girl.
They frowned at the attic's
thousand leather-bound volumes.
The writing was ancient; some on vellum.
The captive they held pleaded and cried
as they made a pile near the road.
"Go ahead" was the command,
petrol ensuring that the fire caught
in a gush of flames
and blackening smoulder.

Waiting

Waiting is what they do. News of skirmishes
gives them no purpose.
Their own mission has yet to arrive,
its timing the shape of an obdurate future.
They talk of growing up in Wangaratta and Hay;
of won football finals; of days
in a swollen river like Huck Finn;
how they farmed and courted;
how Annie rang the church bell
at midnight; of boys who rescued her;
the scandal it caused, the red-face mayor
who stood outraged before a congregation.
Stories repeat. Boredom and anxiety
run fast and stall. Tomorrow, or next month,
they will enter swampland and pass
broken buildings under enemy fire.
Two write letters and three are playing cards.
One sits alone, reading Hemingway.

Court Martial

1.

It had been hijinks at first. We'd been drinking,
Reg had made a speech about barbarism
and how our commanders wouldn't take action.
Some prisoners escaped, a group went after them
and before we knew it Reg had shoved two
out of their cells. Even then, it seemed funny
until he drew his pistol. We stared at them
tumbled on the ground and he shot three others
who were still locked up, talking
about people smiling on the other sides of their faces.
We lumped them in the jeep and buried them
near where the river exits the forest,
falling towards the group of bombed villages.
There was a shrine and ornate statue.
Someone stole that as we were being rounded up.
Reg said it was nothing to do with him.
We said the same. But they looked at us
like we were mongrels. "Better to have told the truth,"
a sergeant said, running a finger across his throat.

2.

That brown river
surging at noon;
wombats digging
holes in the riverbank,
stubborn refusals
backed against daylight;
Amy who roomed
above the sweet shop
with her crippled mother
who stood every morning
at a tall window
sucking the lip
of a willow pattern cup,

while Amy swam
where the river widened
like the pot belly
of a circus fat man.
Birds in high trees
watched bright filaments
fall through boughs,
sitting like councillors
at monthly meetings,
sometimes hopping
as if surprised by a word,
hunching over
grounds of decision.
And school, where Ambrose
insisted that grammar
would put right the world,
Sam who ambled
on palms of hands,
Jane who played chicken
on the old back road,
struck by a car.
Then war and a front
where rats, like small dogs,
worried trenches
and a patrol of nine men
disappeared on a mission—
no remains to return
or bury and grieve for.
After hijinks
and murder of prisoners
it had been like smoke
in front of his eyes—
questions, a need
to make an example,

closing mornings
of fetid, sweet air
pumped out by the jungle,
days of wondering
at the nonsense of life.

Bundle

He lay bundled near dollops of ground,
one arm a rag
hung from a tree.
Men with a stretcher lifted him delicately.
He'd been thrown and curled
where jungle plants,
each one grotesque
nudged the singularity
of his panting flesh.
His hearing was damaged
and language, once ordered,
was as liquid as water.
He saw a thin child absorbed in a game
wandering in a no-go zone
while soldiers watched on,
one lifting his weapon,
squinting and swearing—
he was nine years old.
Someone said "Leave him";
the gun was put down.
Mostly the orderlies left him alone;
a doctor pronounced: "He's soft in the brain",
while eleven ballerinas
danced a scene from *Swan Lake.*
He said "I love you" to the one who danced best
but each night she changed to a flurrying bird
and flew like shrapnel into his head.

Translation

He brought back from war
another life, and had no place to put it.
Black nights followed;
screeches of monkeys
pummelled and bounced
from a jungle's high trees.
"Adjustment" was a doctor's idea
but no therapy
would return the jungle to itself
as it invaded his living room
with tendrils and shouts.
There was boot-polishing drudgery,
unending narrow tracks,
hoppers whirring, and the sound of ticking
just out of sight like a pecking bird,
or someone casually
flicking a holster with a finger.
And patrols, occasional villages
where people farmed
and women fanned away;
or lay as another patrol
had left them; where blossoms
hung like scrotums.
Every prayer he'd tried
had been emptied of gravitas.
The boy he'd found at a swamp's edge
had been eaten by insects—
himself, he'd thought,
in a proximate life. The boy lived on,
stare-eyed and gasping. No doctor
could translate him
or banish his breathing.

And Then Women

walked into streets
wailing, or were ensconced in corridors,
or taken by relatives
into rooms of subdued light.
Men who were left
moved away from parlours and back rooms,
some making statements.
Children were dark-eyed
and had garnered a kind of loathing.
Yet the baker came by in his cart,
shops sold meagre goods,
and light slid down the sky.
When the boys were finally brought back
they were fine boned and their skin shone.
Someone hailed them before shutting his voice down.
Mourners looked at the ground,
or their companions, or the sky
and unspecified distance.

Bombs

One of my father's stories
could have been a parable:
last from a mess hut
in Darwin during the war
he faced a line of Japanese bombs
with the slit trenches' protection
an impossible short distance away.
There was a moment
of seeing his own oblivion,
and, perhaps, because of his lapsed Catholicism,
an aura of an afterlife
as death ambled near
in clumping, explosive steps.
His training had taught him
to lie on the ground
and, after bombs fell either side
and dirt sprayed his helmet,
to the surprise of his mates
he stood up, pale but cheery,
saying something they didn't catch.

Retired General

It had been a success, largely—
battles won, fields conquered.
A career he'd dreamed
playing cowboys and Indians
with a shell-shocked father—
his father's need to outflank him
had often left him in tears.
Now, back home,
he'd been required to cease
barked orders
and finely honed strategies
in the face of bombed houses
and fragments of flesh.
At night, desert winds
rushed through his breathing.

When the Plane Stalled

When the plane stalled
on that final manoeuvre
they'd been cheering the pilot.
Home was a few hours distant.
Time had furrowed towards
the near destination—
girlfriends, beer, a humming piano.
He'd never know whether it was pilot error
or random fire. His parachute
pulled his shoulders upright;
air yelled and hissed. After interrogation
they shot the pilot and navigator;
left him in a cell with gypsies they'd captured.
The guards were efficient.
No-one was allowed to sing.

Mythologies

Lorelei

Escaping from legend
she is becoming
slowly, strongly embodied—
sensing her blood's infusion,
through its copious networks,
feeling thighs tighten.
Her tongue tastes the season's
yeast and pollen, her nose
registers the tang of living water.
Nerves tingle towards sensation;
eyes open to waterlily, reed
and earthy bank; and to the plunge
of birds; the glossy lineaments
of their water-skimming wings.
The thrust of her history—
jilted lover, water spirit, siren of the rock—
becomes a blur, like palpitations
in this unquiet stream,
and her old sense of falling
is now abstract—as is the agony
of high-sung yearning.
Loss still folds inside her
like a fleshly ripple; she is quiet,
knowing it cannot be undone.
Wrecked ships and sailors vanish
like hallucinations. The new year fills her
with keening relief—she'll no longer sing
a part in that old tragedy,
alone and content
in bird-haunted water,
feeling her body's shape,
mouthing her liquid name,
coming alive.

Prometheus

He cannot abandon
this remnant of rock
though the eagle has vanished
and his liver is whole.
Decades passed
yet grasslands still tempt him
with their promise of burning,
and this cleft-seated boulder
has long compelled him
as the place where his youth
was engrossed in pain.
Pandora walked here
with her jar and allure,
maligned by the gods'
ambivalent gifts,
leaving the world
its littered travail,
also superb
in her knowledge and craft—
he remembers her agile
muscular gait,
his Titan heritage
become almost human,
yet his body tightens
with a weird recurrence
of pain in his side.
And this gift, this fire,
that allowed millennia
of smelting and killing—
how to judge its import
or weigh that against
the trickle of red
that runs across grass
when burn-off begins;
that climbs and spreads
like an improbable dance?

Years of hard graft
hang in his body—
even this ladder
has been forged in fire.
He climbs it now
to face the mountain
feeling for something—
perhaps a small bargain
with blackened desire;
and maybe a moment
of watery dousing.

Icarus on Land

for JW

He has tried it in memory
a thousand times—
climbing on wings,
hearing wind-rush
and thrashing feathers,
seeing his prison
fall like an anchor
into blueing distance.
Air sucked his throat;
his skin reflected
the torpor of sunshine.
He had been caught
by an absurd happiness—
being birdlike above
twenty coastlines,
believing that freedom
meant melting the wax
that promised landfall—
he would lift like an eagle
into yellow solitariness,
surveying the world,
and suddenly drop
out of Daedalus' view.
To have survived that fall
made him laugh in wonder
as he careened across stones
and ancient grasses,
feeling his body
primed and ready
in this flurry of pollen
and heated air;
carrying his farmer's
knowledge of soil,
full of the thought
that perhaps once more
he could fly a few metres

if only he practised—
that joy lay chiefly
in wanton persistence.
Bandaged and sore,
rushing at air,
he tries for lift-off.

Ghost Bird

(Mnemosyne)

Each intimation
quizzing the present;
every disturbance
in what we've become—
Mnemosyne sees us
like a ghostly bird,
knowing even
occasions we'd thought
forever gone;
remembers that, young
and still unwary,
we set on fire
a haystack that flared
like a pyre of old.

In a coastal breeze's
airy tide
flames caroused
the length of a field
as a bird took off
from a sparking hedgerow
with wings alight,
turning and fuming
and, Icarus-like,
pausing mid-air
plunged like a comet
head first to the sea.
No cup of Lethe water
will ever unscald it.

Ariadne and the Minotaur

1.
She let him carry fingers
across her torso
until caress dropped
her ground away,
taking her, lurching,
to places she couldn't name
like the darkest words—
a gathering like syllables
cramming her mouth
and the pleasure of incoherence.
She didn't object
to his murmuring babble
or spittle that gathered
at the corner of his mouth
because of his subtle
dawdlings with her body.
She trailed thread
through ritual passages
where annual slaughter
marked the high walls.
He was compelled, she knew it,
from some violence of need.
Many nights she went again
to hear him talk ardently
in jabbering language,
and with gesture when meanings
jagged in his throat,
and through fragments of dance
welling in his body
like an implacable grace.
As he swung around;
as sweat glistened on his chest,
she wanted to taste his salt and skill.

When he idled with her
she believed in his proper name—
Asterion, starlike—
because he brought from her
the sea's lustrous pallor.
She also knew,
as he dandled her arm,
that, half-brother as he was,
she'd betray him
when the sacrifice arrived—
as long as one Greek was brave.
This convulsion of sense
and disarray of being
could not be enough.
She spoke to him once
of wanting solace—
time-without-end—
but he simply bellowed
holding her tightly.
And let her go.

2.
When she returned
she tripped on a bone.
He was languid, as if lost
in memory, pointing
at walls that hemmed them
with Daedalus' craft.
She saw sunlight grip
a flock of white waves
and a girl dip her feet.
There was something beyond her
that Pasiphaë hid;
some motherless part
of his guilt and beauty.

He began to sing
taking her hands,
and she saw him swimming
in hallucination,
holding a child
the colour of sea
that died on the strand.
He said, "She was frightened
and ran into death
like those girded Greeks."
Or that's what she heard
as he snorted and stamped,
conjuring art
in the dirty arena.
He lay a hand
on her intimate body
and rested it there
as if asking a question.

3.
He shuffled daily
through long excursions
into practice and art,
hardly touching her
for a day or a week.
Spitting, thick-tongued
his intractable speech
entranced like a poem,
clogged with itself.
"What if I killed you?"
The words fell idly
and lay on her thigh
where he rested a hand.
He shook his bull head.
"I mean, this dull world…"

They lapsed into quiet
and she washed her hair,
pulling it tight
in a swirling scroll.
He sucked on meat,
spitting out gristle
and, tonguing her arm,
stood up to dance.
Later they walked
through close passageways
to a subtle dead-end.
She heard as if near
the soughing, black sea,
shouts of sailors
and a whip crack expanding.
Asterion shuddered.
She'd lost the thread
to take her back
but he guided her slowly:
"Here, take it up."
A red line to show
what he had relinquished.

Minotaur

1.
Clot-tongued, my speaking was slur.
Mother nursed me. Words
stuck in the tangle-spittle.
Horns butt'd, pricked.
But my body was grace. I,
with tangl'd tongue could entwine-
lose in dance. I roamed
in Daed'lus game. He said,
"Hide-'n'-seek." Gates
clanged-caught—
"Not tame."
"Eat," they said. "Fill-up blood."
But to dance—I kept the turning
season. She taught me—
Pas'phaë, Pha'dra, Ar'adne.
Each was the other. Love.
I lost their diff'rence.
They came, stayed away.

2.
Ar'adne teased, skipped on sand,
hot as blood prickle.
Sea gulped at feet
where cedars reached out
splay-hand roots.
The world blood-colour—
ol'ander rose-bitt'r,
hibis-cus blush. We scrambl'd
in gorges. I held—
back on rock, panting eyes—
and she pushed:
"Don't dare."
The mount'n stood up
blear-shade.

That was "once upon time"
before Daed'lus.
Mother sat me:
"You're old."

3.
Thought was slow,
then to do.
But no gap
on lab'rinth green
that Daed'lus made
for my dance.
All me in feet and tumble,
swiv'l jump, arm-grace,
head-high.
Ar'adne, I
gorging rhythm.
Pha'dra, I
gorging rhythm.
They me, I them,
lifted.

4.
Dread-sense
as if Ar'adne made
a dance-death—
"Your sis would never."
Laugh-look.
"Theseus is strong."
I nuzzl'd her breast
and she stepped.
Back in lab'rinth night,
chink of grill.
A murmur
of coming-to-meet.

I hid, saw as Ar'adne—
handsome and quick,
sure-shifting,
his quick-switching sword
like a partner
dressed
in soft gath'r glitt'r.

Spider: prose poems

Spider

In sweeping up leaves he disturbed a spider that ran across his shoe. Forty years ago, the same occurrence. His father flicked it from his bare foot and carried him to the car. A journey to the beach, sand and waves like kinks of ice-cream. That brilliant sea crashing against a groyne. A girl in yellow bathers who smiled. His brother and sister bickering. And an almost translucent spider that his father gathered, running whitely on his tanned, outstretched hand.

Jars
for PM

1. Wingcloth

He kept insects in them, wings glinting in summer light like a kind of fabric—wingcloth, dressing the backs of elves. He never kept larkspur in fruit jars but that was in a novel and he imagined intense, clustering flowers leaning against cloudy glass rims. He used jars for rolled manuscripts, lined up on his jarrah desk. They were his only typed copies, before computers—poems and stories to be unscrewed and read. He kept memories, too—creatures let out at night. They climbed walls and ran across his eiderdown when his parents had left the room. Sometimes he screwed those lids impossibly tight.

2. Pterodactyl

Jars were rooms for model dinosaurs and dolls, insects, grass straggles, spasms of light. Unseemly mists climbed through microclimates. Inside larger jars twigs became giant redwoods; spawnings of worms and grubs writhed in bottles with pierced lids. Years later, digging the garden, his parents came across a cache of jars filled with dirt and stains. One contained a dissolved specimen from a biology lab. What had it been? A baby mammal; an exotic reptile like the pterodactyl in the museum from the Bavarian forests, fingerbone-wings curled against glassy hardening? He'd thrown the jar back and forth on the school oval with a friend, hearing preserving liquid slosh, hiding it as contraband.

3. Plague

A plague of cicadas. He could barely heft it home after showing the class—a biology project that was all *tour de force* and little practicality. To get them had been to sweat and clamber for hours on a windless Saturday. After two decades underground they had come to this—scooped into paper bags, dropped into bottles, poured into one large jar. Three days later they were dead and had never shrilled (he knew the ancient Greeks venerated their sound). Tipping them into a bin he marvelled at how small their mass had become, that had clambered and filled the jar's interior with plump refractions. Their dark bodies seemed unused to daylight. Why don't you shrill? he thought, tipping out the last one.

4. Eden

The large glass container was a tank for Beatrice and Dante, shiny goldfish from the pet shop. They swam in murky water, nibbling weeds and titbits thrown in. One day both were belly up. With thin schoolboy arm twisting into the bottle's neck he achingly scrubbed algae and slime, making a bed for spider plants. He created a glass-skied Eden, placing two plastic figures at the front. The plants grew wildly in enriched pond dirt; the figures grew mildewed with time and stasis. Sometimes he imagined the fish still there, making good in clear water—if only he'd known how to keep them; if knowledge had been enough.

5. Janie

On that beach holiday we filled jars with seawater (seeing how, close up, it lost its blue) and tendrilled writhings of seaweed, volute shells, white sand, grey sand, variegated pebbles, cuttlebones, white egg-shaped pebbles, sliding crabs. We made beach scenes in miniature, lining them up on the shore; listened to windy swell inside shells, sucked sauce from corned-beef sandwiches, climbed rock ledges. Our parents sunbaked, swam, told us to "play". Janie, the skinny daughter of a professor, on loan to us while they travelled, teetered on a ledge until the sea washed her away. We dived after her white body and pulled her in where she coughed up seawater and vomit. She showed us a journal entry her mother had written about life being a cage or jar, and how she would break it to pieces. We remembered our own jars, running to inspect them, but the tide had surged and they were nowhere to be seen—except one that held a bluebottle, careening in the wash. Later that year we saw Janie at a camp. Her mother had gone away, she said, and her father sobbed every night in his room. She gestured with widening hands as if there was nothing to secure her, like a jar taken by the tide.

Notebooks

When she found her mother's notebooks in the shed in the back garden, their pages were stuck together with age and dirt; light had yellowed them, insects had mottled and eaten them. She threw them in the skip along with so much desultory-looking furniture, not even bothering to prise the pages apart. What, after all, had her mother ever done? A handful of committees, work, those few friends she kept to herself. Some of the notebooks landed on top of a writing desk. It seemed almost poignant—that they might lie for a few more hours where they were written. Days later, after the skip was gone, she regretted her casualness—two notebooks lay on the grass. She took them inside and a page fell open. "And then to love in this way—it has been completely unexpected…" She read every page, jemmying them apart with a knife, exposing pain and ardour. Her mother was a stranger. Her words were of someone else's life.

Reading

Under the deck rolls of chicken wire were a nascent hen yard and spiders made home there. Sophie and I brought rugs and cushions, making it our own small habitat, cuddling and talking—at twelve that seemed perfect. Sometimes her cat passed and once a lizard watched us from a dry-stone wall. During a staring summer she read *Little Dorrit* in clear, sensuous tones, halting at words she didn't understand. I scanned the dictionary as she spelled out each one. Two years later we kissed and clamped legs. "I do, but I don't." We read *Lady Chatterley*, touching hands.

Wave

There's a picture of a giant wave above the mantelpiece in the old bedroom. As frozen as those lovers on Keats' urn. It came early last century in a packing crate, was framed badly, yet it lives in the room like the breath of fire. It has been years since anyone stirred the grate; renovations have isolated the room, yet somewhere in the wainscotting time is marked by small noises. The house seems to lean towards this bedroom, as if a wave once shifted foundations. An intimate letter drifts on the wide sea of the floor.

Memory Gardens

They were not real, of course—those places you took me to. The statue in the square based on a lost Leonardo drawing; the cafe serving *spaghetti all'arrabbiata*; the poorly lit gallery with two masterpieces from the medieval period. And that ruin of a monastery with a grove of oranges in its central quadrangle. I believed in them at the time, and you embraced me, saying "This is living." Later we went to a house of mirrors and a hilltop garden. Children ran past. The vista showed a ruined house, which we approached. I saw myself in a playground; I saw you climbing a tree, no more than twelve years old. I turned towards a man carrying balloons and he pointed to a garden behind a wall. I knew then that this was memory, unreal as a fable. You were dressed in green and reading philosophy in a time before I knew you.

Lost

What I lost was not what I thought. I'd believed loss lay chiefly in the absence of things we made and shared—small trays inlaid with mosaics, piles of clean washing, elaborate salads in large bowls. And in conversation's absence. But something else was missing and one day I saw it like a woman standing in my room—the way another body had meshed with my body through a thousand unnamed proximities. An unstated belief that we belonged together even in our alienations. And a constancy of gesture, as if handing the other space; as if letting the other's space settle and run through hands.

Wedding Dress

The old fabric began to come apart as she manoeuvred the dress carefully down her torso. From the old photographs she was convinced that her size was right but lace came away and hemstitching pulled. Her mother had refused to wear it, preferring black slacks at a registry office. As a girl this had saddened her—to know the white dress had been there, handed down. She sucked in her stomach and the dress fitted. She stood in front of the mirror and imagined herself in the nineteenth century. Would that have been better—to be a possession; to be given away? She peeled fabric back over her head. Her grandmother had been escorted down the aisle by a father who later disowned her—something about propriety and family. The local paper reported her grandmother as resplendent. She stood in her underwear and thought, yes, a few alterations, phoning her best friend. "Bring green dye," she said. "Bring pinking shears."

Time

If this room were made of skin; if the structure was bones and blood; we would hear a heartbeat rattling our ears. If we lay next to ribbons of veins and arteries, and muscles that constrained them, we'd feel a rush and slow return like a merging of red and blue. Knowledge would not be of news broadcasts and disrupted worlds, but of what reiterated day by day—a universal mantra; a deep concatenation of background breathing. One week we may look up and see a clock we'd hung. Its face would be a hand crawling across strange rhythms. We might call it the world. We might live in that time.

Cut Waterlily Flower

for RR

1.

The cut waterlily flower was upright in its vase, with peeping purple suggestions. We watched it for days and it wouldn't unfold; moved it into lacquering sunshine; scrutinised its water. Swamplands, lily ponds, impressionist paintings passed under our gaze. A white hat careened from a balcony. The lily's stalk bent a little, as if in the act of genuflecting. The flower was a closed eye; and so many notions that hadn't come to fruition. It was an instrument that withheld its notes. We circled it in silence, sensing we had so much more to say.

2.

Finally it began to blossom—slowly, like someone waking. Day after day its subtle tissue-paper purple offered small aspects and interleavings. Tidily, it yawned but would not fully open its mouth. We interrogated it, holding cups of tea close, cajoling it like an intimate. You bent and kissed it, as if on the lips. Next day the dark stalk was handhold for a flare; you carried it about the room. The day afterwards it signalled distress, flecked by tears. That was four days ago and its flame was all glory. Today it has begun to fade and we admire what we remember it was. How it was nascent for so long, like something entombed; how it surprised us. We remember the dark stalk we trimmed; and the imperturbability it held, like a species of consideration. Now, caught in the glass, we see its reflection like smeared lipstick.

Octopus

When he picked up the jar with a live blue-ringed octopus, it looked benign, as if death might be a form of prettiness. His father said "put it down, boy" as if death might simply be gathered and let go. Later, there was something beautiful in the thought—that his father knew when to leave: "I have decided to die," he said. The blue-ringed octopus might have been in his father's hand. Nearly immobile at the end, he kept faith with matter-of-factness, and cradled love like a familiar. Let me hold him again, he thought as he left the hospital. And: never let me hold him again.

Pictures at an exhibition 2

Painting 11: *Crucible*

Is this a mirror for an indelicate life,
a narrative of wasteful memory
and clotted desire? Does the chase
through penumbral woods
to three saints' assassination,
gold-leafed haloes undimmed
by daggers and axe,
signify, in my agnostic house,
a bleak, unadmitted wish?
At the back of the painting
can that figure be me
looking over his shoulder, slinking away,
bent over a little, searching for a coin?
The sun is dreary
and the murderous woods
are clear of birds. The figure balances
an alchemist's crucible
in the crook of an arm.

Painting 12: *Language*

Today it is strewn with words,
the painting named, like a catalogue;
every image finding a counterpart
in language; so a yellow slash of sun
is a scrawl I can barely decipher—
"banana" it may be—as if I've misread
the brushstrokes for years;
as if this fire and light is, after all,
a bowl of raddled fruit.
"Mountain", the painting says bluntly,
"stone", "stream". I miss the way
images gushed and frothed.
"Waterfall" it states
but little occurs.
"Vista" reveals nothing.

Painting 13: *Excursion*

Words drip like viscous wax.
Refusing to dry
they smear the image.
"Stone" slides to "s",
"house" blurs to grey
and "the apple grove"
crawls with worm-like descenders,
fallen apples
lying brownly in grass.
Yet a strong willow stays
where I might teeter outwards,
hand-sliding on boughs,
tearing skin
and landing upright—
and there, improbably,
next to still water,
light's an excursion
into what might be real.

Painting 14: *Fluctuations*

Its soft fluctuations
are like a body
rising at morning
with the opaque investment
that light possesses
before clarity accosts it—
the landscape a puzzle
about what we'd see
if we could see better.
At night it's quizzical,
becoming abstract,
as if a clock
has forgotten to turn
and, mounting a bicycle
with muddy tyres—
burnt umber, some grey
and a highlight of water—
there's a sideways back road
where old elms queue stiffly.
I step from the bike
and there, in sun splashes,
are names I'd lost
for intractable things,
scumbled in thought
as sticky as grass.

Painting 15: *Trustees*

A gathering of portraits
in suits and stern faces
looks like trustees
of contemporary belonging:
keepers of manuscripts;
guardians of archives;
curators possessing
hoards of treasure.
Gravitas becomes them
as if memory, like size,
or like a cobwebbed sheen,
is brushed on the canvases
their faces slanted
with yesterday's gaze.
One holds a tool
without blade or sharp point;
another a costume
of outlandish colour;
a third points at photos
of domed, ancient buildings,
as if beneath varnish
they murmur together:
"Do not forget
the human strangeness."

Painting 16: *Sky and Tree*

This is brusque—after all
it will not know
a non-rectangled view
or frameless vista.
I try to see past
insistent perspectives.
That tree, leaning a little
and bending feathering leaves,
might be sipping at the lake—
or it's a dipping heron.
This dark-bricked house
is where we grew up, shoving each other.
And there are words I nearly hear
forever receding—
"love", "enough", "never".

Painting 17: *Squirrel*

for LD

Each hair in the brush
is a thought in the squirrel;
each brushstroke a bound
into trees where nuts
are stored for winter.
Each deposit of paint
is a month or long year
when the squirrel has felt
the rain on its nose;
wind rattles leaves
and the storehouse of being
empties a little.
The painting thinks
with an animal's instinct;
wakes at night
with squirrel eyes;
searches long vistas
of grassland and forest,
sniffs at air
for what might arrive.

Painting 18: *Curtain*
for RR

A yellow curtain twitches above a bed
with calligraphic patterns, like a script
to tell of omens. Halting words
like abstract, geometric plants—
Akkadian or Sumerian it must be—
are climbing into image out of prayer
chasing the ineffable; or lovers' talk
is inching towards light in syllables.
Where the curtain gapes, bluish glass
suggests a distant city—conversation
near a petrol pump; jags of weather;
and distant, revving bikes
as persistent as a migraine starting.
Inside the room a bedspread keeps an imprint
of a gasping couple beneath a fan—
one said a word that made the other blush;
they left a book and ruffled, silken scarf
like implications of their spoken touch.

Painting 19: *Hills*

Last week I cut the painting
from the frame of my eyes—
blue tussocks, wind, red house.
It had walked into memory
extruding being like messy pigment—
a life in a murderous place
I wouldn't own up to.
An infant wailed in grass;
a man with uncertain intentions
shrugged heavy shoulders
while I babbled a language I didn't know.
I see it like yesterday—
this painting, its life that assumed mine,
a woman somewhere outside the frame
who wished to claim me.
So I cut the painting away
and it lies with folds
in the back of the canvas
like small hills—that white, unprimed surface
hiding a picture that faces a wall.
I have begun to miss it badly.

Painting 20: *Robes*

It moved a little, to scrutinise him,
eyeing him like a judge
and he knew it found him wanting.
He'd been too passionate,
full of his own grief—
the painting thought that indelicate.
In the background there was a scene
of lovers in a boat on a European canal.
Both were dressed in elegant clothes
and on the shore a robed official
was waiting to greet them.
The woman dipped her hand in water.
The man seemed absurdly happy
as she adjusted her hat
and briefly looked away.

Painting 21: *Black Dress*

for TAW

This black dress
is also a painting—
it hangs on a wall
where light holds it close.
It's a doorway to places
no-one quite knows;
that bloom and rain
with extravagant vistas.

We've sometimes entered
into the painting
dipping dark hats,
watching children
riding down lanes
(their slit-eyed scrutiny
prickling our backs),
finding a house
made out of art—
colourful images; chaotic signs—
and in a long room
have seen a black dress.

Approaching the work
we've watched ourselves there,
climbing through streetscapes,
avoiding riders
and ducking rain,
entering a house
made out of painting,
finding a room
with a black dress inside.

Now standing here,
outside of the image,
the dress seems mute

hung on its wall;
yet inside the painting,
through folds like a curtain,
we glimpse narrow laneways.
The sound of rain
is prickling our backs.

Painting 22: *Portrait of a Count*

for my father

Italians might say
this painting's an aristocrat
surveying his world.
But he also looks inward
toward his own death—
centuries ago
he was buried in Rome.
I try to connect
with his intimate gaze
as his dark velvet cloak
falls away from the frame
like a dying tide.
It might be my father
in a different era
(he always loved clothes),
sinking and settling
towards dark earth
as if soil is dragging
his gait to a grave.
The painting's tones
are astonishingly lifelike—
how those pigments have shone
through centuries—
yet now there's craquelure
dividing the flesh.
I see my father
living an afterlife
as a picture of someone
he never encountered—
and then he's suddenly
gone from the room.
Italians might say
he was never there;
that this is a Count
from old Roman times;

and I would believe them
except for the gaze
that quizzes me now
with my father's eyes.

ACKNOWLEDGMENTS

Poems in this collection, some in different form, have previously appeared in the following publications:

Aesthetica Creative Writing Annual 2015: "Furniture"
Aesthetica Creative Writing Annual 2014: "Angels at Nedlands Primary School, 1968"
Australian Book Review's States of Poetry anthology (ACT) (ed. Jen Webb): "Black Dress", "Eyes", "River"
The Best Australian Poems 2015: "What Was Left"
The Best Australian Poems 2014: "Fox"
The Canberra Times: "Burnt Umber", "Wave"
Cordite 51.1: UMAMI: "What Was Left"
Fire: A Collection of Stories, Poems and Visual Images (ed. Delys Bird): "Bushfire"
Global Poetry Anthology 2013 (Montreal Poetry prize shortlist anthology): "House"
Jars (chapbook: Canberra: Authorised Theft, 2015) "Wingcloth", "Pterodactyl", "Plague", "Eden", "Janie", "Octopus"
New Writing: The International Journal for the Practice and Theory of Creative Writing: "Notebooks", "Reading"
Six Different Windows, Crawley: UWA Publishing, 2013: "Bombs"
The Stars Like Sand: Australian Speculative Poetry: "A Museum of the Future"
TEXT: Journal of Writing and Writing Courses: "Minotaur"
Toasted Cheese (US): "Roadways"
Viscera: Poems (chapbook: Canberra: Dancing Scorpion Press, 2014): "Trench", "Sun Bursts", "Meeting", "Dropped Book", "Burning the Books", "Waiting", "Court Martial", "Bundle", "Translation", "And Then Women", "Bombs", "Retired General", "When the Plane Stalled"
Westerly: "Squirrel", "Five Occasions of Water"
Western Humanities Review (US): "Rooftop"
Writing to the Wire anthology (ed. Dan Disney and Kit Kelen): part one of the poem "Refugees", published under the title "Visitors"

The "Viscera" poems were part of the exhibition *Viscera* (contributing artists: Paul Hetherington and Jen Webb) exhibited at Manning Clark House, 11 Tasmania Circle, Forrest ACT 2603, 2–14 November 2014.

The poems "Lorelei", "Prometheus", "Icarus on Land" and "Ghost Bird" were part of the exhibition *Nearly Birds* (contributing artists: Judith Crispin, Victoria Royds and Paul Hetherington) exhibited at Belconnen Arts Centre, 118 Emu Bank, Belconnen ACT 2617, 18 January – 3 February 2013; and at Photonet Gallery, 15a Railway Place, Fairfield Vic 3078, 5–25 May 2013.

Thanks to everyone who helped me write the poems in this book, particularly: Michelle Hetherington and our daughters, Suzannah and Rebecca; Ian Templeman, Lucy Dougan, Cassandra Atherton, Jen Webb, Judith Crispin, Maggie Shapley, Rachel Robertson, Paul Munden, Katharine Coles, Andrew Melrose, Tom Stillinger, Hephzibah Rendle-Short, Bella Li, Maureen Brooks, Julian Stannard, Antonia Pont, Anne Caldwell, Penelope Layland, Shane Strange, Caren Florance, Monica Carroll, Romola Templeman and Angelina Russo. Thanks to all members of the International Poetry Studies Institute's Prose Poetry Writing Group, who stimulated the production of various prose poems in this collection, and to Molonglo Writers Group members for years of inspiration and collegiality.

I am very grateful to the Literature Section of the Australia Council for awarding me a six-month Residency in the BR Whiting Studio in Rome, during which time I worked on this publication.

And thanks especially to Terri-ann White—an exemplary publisher—and the rest of the highly supportive UWA Publishing team.